THE NATIONAL TRUST
Dyrham Park

Dyrham Park
A modest grandeur

When you turn off the Bath–Stroud road, you leave the roar of modern traffic behind you. The drive curves down between herds of quietly grazing deer, which gave their name to the place centuries ago (Dyrham means 'an enclosed valley frequented by deer' in Old English). Then, you get your first, unforgettable sight of the house.

Dyrham Park may be grand architecture, but its setting is modest, buried into the valley slopes below. It was all the vision of one man: WILLIAM BLATHWAYT, an ambitious, but rather prosaic, civil servant, who made his fortune by marrying well and acquiring lucrative jobs in the government of William III. Between 1692 and 1704 he gradually transformed an existing Tudor house into a mansion in the already old-fashioned baroque style, and filled it with Dutch pictures, china and furniture.

Blathwayt had built a country house fit for a dynasty of aristocrats, but his descendants were content to take his name and remain ordinary Gloucestershire squires. They had neither the money nor the imagination to modernise the house, and lived lightly on the surface of the place. So it has survived as a rare and remarkably complete example of late 17th-century Dutch-influenced taste.

Only two people have made changes since – both outsiders. In the 1840s COLONEL BLATHWAYT saved Dyrham from dismemberment, sympathetically redecorating the family rooms and modernising the rambling servants' quarters. In 1938–46 the tenant ANNE, LADY ISLINGTON repainted the Drawing Room and the Walnut Staircase in the light colours fashionable at the time.

The builder of Dyrham ran William III's army, and his descendants fought at Waterloo and on the Somme. So it was fitting that the house and park should come to the nation in 1956 through the National Land Fund, which had been founded as a memorial to the dead of the Second World War. The National Trust tries to preserve the tranquil, but fragile, spirit of Dyrham in their memory.

If you would like to know more about Dyrham, try the audio guide, or buy the CD-ROM, which provides a virtual tour of the house and a detailed description of its contents.

William Blathwayt,
the builder of the house

(*Below*) The painted overdoors in the Balcony Room are typical of Dyrham's late 17th-century decoration

The Blathwayt family on the west terrace around 1880. Captain George Blathwayt (standing at the back in the white hat) kept a brief diary of his quiet life at Dyrham: '*1 January 1852*: Seedy after the Oyster Supper; 2: Stag hounds met at Wick; 3: Carriage to Bath; 4: Took some Phisick [medicine], walked through the Park; 5: Gallop in the Park before Breakfast'

Tour of the House

The West Hall. By the fireplace is a dummy board, which has been here since at least 1703. These cut-out figures painted on wooden panels seem to have first appeared in English houses in the late 17th century. Favourite subjects included elegantly dressed men and women, pedlars and servants with brooms

(*Opposite*) The Great Hall. Blathwayt, who was an avid book collector, kept part of his huge library in the pair of glazed bookcases flanking the door to the Dining Room. They are almost identical to those made in 1666 for the diarist Samuel Pepys by Thomas Sympson, a master joiner in the Deptford dockyards. However, only one is original (on the left); the other is a replica made in 1927

The West Hall

This was the modest entrance hall for the new suite of rooms that William Blathwayt added to the house in 1692–4. It was a place of constant comings and goings, and so was built of hard-wearing materials, with panelled walls and a large black marble fireplace to keep it warm. The floor here is heavily worn, and you can still see the lead plugs in the floor (left of the fireplace) where Lady Islington inserted a partition in the 1930s.

The Dutch character of Dyrham is clear right from the start. The Cromwellian chairs are covered with Dutch leather. The landscape paintings hanging on the walls are by minor 17th-century Dutch artists and still have their original Dutch-style black frames. The tile pictures of exotic palms and pineapples flanking the fireplace were manufactured in Delft, and were inspired by a Dutch East India Company expedition to China. Dummy boards, like that here of a maid peeling an apple, probably originated in the Low Countries.

Entrance halls were traditionally where you stored weapons so that they would be ready to hand in time of trouble. Those shown here include a collection of 18th- and 19th-century swords and bayonets and (in the case on the table) a rare pair of holster pistols, which Blathwayt probably took on campaign with William III in Flanders.

The Great Hall

This huge space is the historic core of Dyrham. It was the Great Hall in the early Tudor house and is all that survives from that building after it was remodelled by William Blathwayt; his portrait may be seen in the room.

Although Blathwayt no longer dined with his servants as they did in medieval times, he still wanted an impressive room in which to receive important guests, and to host balls and musical evenings. So he laid a sprung floor of Flemish oak for dancing, and would have pushed the furniture back against his new panelled walls, just as it is today. He also played billiards here. His younger son, John, whose portrait hangs to the right of the fireplace, was a brilliant harpsichordist in his youth, and Dyrham's musical tradition is maintained with regular outdoor concerts in the summer. The south-facing windows and the late 18th-century Irish crystal chandeliers ensure that it receives plenty of light. The French flock wallpaper was put up in the mid-19th century, and the panelling was first painted white in 1938 and last redecorated in 1978.

The three ceiling paintings by the 18th-century Italian artist Andrea Casali depict Architecture and Astronomy, History and Time, Music and Painting. Originally from Fonthill Splendens in Wiltshire (which appears in the painting by the window), they were incorporated into the decoration of the Theatre Royal, Bath, and in 1845 bought by Col. Blathwayt for Dyrham.

To the left of the fireplace hangs *An Urchin mocking an Old Woman eating Polenta* by the Spanish artist Bartolomé Murillo (1618–82). Murillo's depictions of street life in his native Seville were particularly popular with foreign collectors like Thomas Povey, from whom William I Blathwayt may have acquired this picture. In 1765 his grandson William was forced to sell the painting to pay creditors, and acquired the copy now hanging on the facing wall to fill the gap. However, his brother stepped in to buy the original, which later returned to Dyrham, hence the pair

Table layout for a dinner in 1822

The Dining Room

This room was created only in the late 18th century, when a parlour and an adjoining closet were combined to make a larger space for formal dining. Throughout the 18th century, the Blathwayts seem to have managed without a room set aside specifically for eating. In 1844–5 the Kitchen was moved from the far end of the servants' block to a more convenient position in the basement, under the windows of the Great Hall (see p.19). The Dining Room faces north, and so gets no sun, but the Victorians preferred to eat in the shade.

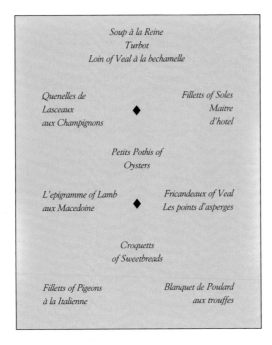

Soup à la Reine
Turbot
Loin of Veal à la bechamelle

Quenelles de
Lasceaux
aux Champignons

Filletts of Soles
Maitre
d'hotel

Petits Pothis of
Oysters

L'epigramme of Lamb
aux Macedoine

Fricandeaux of Veal
Les points d'asperges

Croquetts
of Sweetbreads

Filletts of Pigeons
à la Italienne

Blanquet de Poulard
aux trouffes

The portrait to the right of the fireplace depicts William Blathwayt's uncle and mentor, Thomas Povey, in 1658. Two years later, Povey became an influential, if rather incompetent, official in Charles II's government. He was also a collector of taste, whom the diarist John Evelyn called 'a nice contriver of all elegancies'. In 1693 Blathwayt bought books and 112 pictures from Povey's collection, many of which are still at Dyrham. They include, over the fireplace, the portrait of the Restoration playwright Thomas Killigrew, who built the first Theatre Royal in Drury Lane, London, and *A Boy with a Greyhound* (a copy after Van Dyck), which hangs opposite the fireplace.

The Drawing Room

Today, this room reflects the taste of the widowed Anne, Lady Islington, who rented Dyrham from 1938 to 1946. She disliked the sombre brown interiors of the house and tried to lighten them up in the style of the time. In 1938 she converted this room into a drawing room, painting the fireplace and the dark-grained woodwork white. The 18th-century Italian-style wallpaper was put up in the 1960s by the Trust.

Originally, this was a family parlour with gilt leather wallhangings like those still in the East Hall. Here, the family would have assembled every Sunday morning: the door to the left of the fireplace conceals a covered passage leading to the family pew in the church. By 1839 the room had been converted into a library.

The Drawing Room, which was redecorated by Lady Islington in the 1930s

The Walnut Staircase

The Walnut Staircase forms the starting point for the first of the two sets of state apartments you will see at Dyrham. The idea of creating a linked suite of formally furnished rooms came from the French court of Louis XIV. By the late 17th century it was being adopted in the more ambitious new English country houses like Dyrham. A grand staircase led up to an ante-room, a bedroom, and, finally, to a pair of small closets, each more lavishly decorated and more private than the last. In the royal court, your social status determined exactly how far you were allowed to penetrate such apartments. In country houses, they were generally used to receive or accommodate important visitors. Increasingly, however, they fell out of daily use, instead becoming 'rooms of parade', through which guests would process, enjoying the decoration and furnishings, much like the modern-day visitor.

The Walnut Staircase is part of the new west range that William Blathwayt added to the house in 1692–4. Since 1680 he had been auditor-general for the British colony of Virginia, and it was Virginia walnut that he chose for the stairs and banisters of his new staircase. Blathwayt rejected one design for the banisters, objecting that 'this will harbour dust very much'. The wainscot was first painted white, then, in 1844–5, a dark red, and the present grey and gold by Lady Islington in 1946. Note the particularly fine French-style parquet floor on the half-landings.

The staircase is dominated by Samuel van Hoogstraeten's *Perspective View of a Courtyard*, which was much admired by Thomas Povey's friend Samuel Pepys.

The Balcony Room

This was the ante-room or private sitting room to the Tapestry Bedroom next door and occupies the key central position above the west entrance door. The architectural panelling, made by Robert Barker of London about 1693, emphasizes its importance. The dark walnut graining looks authentically 17th-century, but in fact was added in the mid-19th century. The original effect was even grander: the walls were painted to resemble marble, the columns gilt and porphyry (a dark red speckled stone). The red and white marble chimneypiece was only moved here from the East Hall in 1938. But the Oriental tea-table and the candlestands, supported by chained black slaves, were in this room by 1700. The stands belonged originally to Povey, who, like Blathwayt, derived part of his wealth from administering the slave plantations of Jamaica. Blathwayt himself appears to have had very little involvement in the slave trade, although in the 18th century, nearby Bristol was second only to Liverpool in its promotion of the transatlantic trade in slaves.

The 1703 inventory records 'a fflowerpot in ye Chimny of Delf' in this room. The blue-and-white Delft vase in the fireplace today is filled with an arrangement of cut-silk flowers inspired by the 17th-century Dutch and French flower paintings in this room. As in the pictures, the arrangements combine flowers that would never naturally be in bloom together.

Take time to look at the brass door locks in the Balcony Room. The decoration is again floral: daffodils, chrysanthemums, strawberries, tulips and roses. Blathwayt probably bought the locks from the London showroom of Henry Walton, whose business card is on display in the Justice Room. They were made about 1694 by John Wilkes of Birmingham, which was already a thriving centre for metal-working. Locks were an essential precaution to protect such richly furnished rooms. The keys would have been held by Blathwayt's unmarried sister Elizabeth, who acted as his housekeeper after the death of his wife

The Balcony Room

The Tapestry Bedchamber

Blathwayt seems to have intended this as his own bedroom, but never to have slept here. His wife Mary had died in 1691, before work on the new house had begun, and he kept this room as a shrine to her, complete with her combs, brushes and pin cushions.

The 17th-century Flemish tapestries give this room its special richness, but they also had a practical function – to keep the drafts out and the warmth in. They have also been treated somewhat brutally over the years, more than once being cut up to fit the space, like wallpaper, and moved around the house. They depict the fountains and parterres of the famous mid-17th-century gardens at Enghien near Brussels.

The Colonel's Bedroom

Colonel Blathwayt created this room in 1844–5 as a large bedroom for himself, and this arrangement has been restored. Originally, the space comprised no fewer than four small rooms, which formed the climax of the first-floor apartment: the Japan Closet (furnished with a japanned, or lacquered, table), the Clouded Room (named after the 'clouded silk' hangings), the Striped Plush Room and an Anteroom, where a servant slept so as to be on hand if his master required him during the night. The back stairs led down from here to the servants' quarters.

Pass through the lobby, which was the bedroom used by Colonel Blathwayt's Irish wife, Marianne, and descend the Nursery Stairs.

The Nursery Corridor

During her brief married life, Mary Blathwayt had four children, three of whom survived infancy. They occupied the bedrooms off this corridor. The house menu books for the 1820s reveal that the children ate the same food as the servants. These rooms were kept especially busy after 1850 by the Colonel's grandchildren.

Continue down the next short flight of stairs, and turn left in the corridor and then left into the Justice Room.

The Justice Room

As a leading local landowner, the owner of Dyrham was almost automatically appointed a JP, and until 1848 he was allowed to try cases at home. It was in this room, on the servants' side of the house, that these trials were held. Dyrham itself was not immune from crime. On the night of 23 April 1817 'some evil disposed Person or Persons' broke into the house through the Orangery and 'cut off the covers of a sofa and four chairs of rich figured red velvet'. A £20 reward was offered for information leading to their arrest.

The room is now used to display a changing exhibition about life at Dyrham, drawn from the rich Blathwayt archives.

The Print Room

The Blathwayts used this room as their day-to-day dining room. The deal panelling is hung with a collection of late 17th- and 18th-century portrait engravings, some of which are Dutch. The painted portrait may be of Mary Blathwayt's grandfather, Sir George Wynter (d.1638).

The walnut and tortoiseshell chest-on-stand in the Tapestry Room was probably made by Dutch craftsmen working in London around 1700. Blue-and-white china is displayed on top of it in the fashion of the time

The Print Room, which the family used as their everyday dining room

The Tapestry Bedchamber

The Siege of La Rochelle in 1628, which hangs below the Cedar Stairs, depicts Louis XIII's army surrounding the port city, which was being held by rebel French Protestants

The Cedar Staircase

(Opposite) Samuel van Hoogstraeten's illusionistic *A View down a Corridor* has been hung in a doorway, as it was meant to be viewed

Re-cross the Great Hall and enter the door to the right of the Dining Room door. You are now in the east range, which was added by the royal architect William Talman between 1698 and 1702.

The Cedar Staircase

This room mirrors the Walnut Staircase on the west side of the house, but is altogether grander in scale, rising to the most lavish apartment in the house, which was on the first floor (now dismantled and not shown to visitors), and also to the second floor. By this stage, Blathwayt had even greater ambitions for Dyrham, hoping to impress the new monarch, Queen Anne, whom he expected would visit. In the event, she never did.

The balusters, stair risers and carved brackets were all made from American cedar, while the dado, the underside of the staircase, the doors and the window cases were painted to match. The stair treads are

again Virginia walnut. The painted marbling on the walls is 19th-century.

The picture under the stairs shows the siege of La Rochelle in 1628. Charles I tried to help the French Protestants who were defending the port against their own king, but his expedition ended in humiliating failure. That on the landing is of the siege of Tangier in 1683. Charles II had acquired this north African town in 1662 on his marriage to the Portuguese Catherine of Braganza, and appointed Povey as its treasurer. But it proved impossible to defend from the Moorish army shown in the foreground and was abandoned in 1684.

From the Cedar Staircase, you can look into the Library.

The Library

Lady Islington turned this into a library in 1938. Originally, it had been decorated with Scottish tartan wall-hangings, and in the 19th century it became the billiard room. Through the door on the far side of the room you can see Samuel van Hoogstraeten's *A View down a Corridor*. It was painted in 1662, when the artist was visiting London, but depicts an unmistakably Dutch interior. Pepys saw it in Povey's London house: 'I do most admire his piece of perspective especially, he opening me the closet door and there I saw that there is nothing but only a plain picture hung upon the wall.' The picture has been hung in exactly the same way to bring out the illusion, which is best appreciated by looking back from further on in your tour.

The pair of Dutch Delftware pyramid vases was made in the 1680s–90s, when the craze for collecting this kind of blue-and-white china, led by Queen Mary, was at its height. They were used mainly for displaying tulips, which had enjoyed an even more intense period of popularity in the 1630s. 'Tulipomania' drove collectors to pay huge sums for a single bulb that might produce the much-prized variegated flowers.

Detail of the embossed leather hangings in the East Hall, which have darkened greatly with age

The East Hall

This hall forms the centre of Talman's east range, mirroring the West Hall on the opposite side of the Great Hall. From here, Blathwayt and his guests would have stepped out into his formal water garden, which was swept away in the late 18th century.

Blathwayt bought the embossed leather wall-hangings in The Hague. They cost about 5s a skin and were hung here during the unusually damp summer of 1702, which made them more flexible to work with. These hangings were almost certainly

made in Amsterdam. Leather made an attractive wall-covering which was more hard-wearing than fabric and less likely to harbour smells.

In 1938 Lady Islington inserted the fireplace and painted the cedar panelling white, most of which has now been restored.

The paintings of poultry, turkeys, geese and shelduck are all by the late 17th-century Dutch artist Melchior de Hondecoeter, who specialised in painting birds in garden settings.

You now enter the ground-floor state apartment, which comprised four rooms.

The Diogenes Room

This was built as the ante-room to the bedchamber beyond, but by the 19th century it had become unfashionable to have bedrooms on the ground floor, and they were converted into drawing rooms.

The room takes its name from the Diogenes tapestries, which were made either in the Mortlake or Soho factories in the late 17th century. That on the wall to the right of the fireplace depicts Alexander the Great meeting the philosopher Diogenes, who lived an austere life in a barrel. When Alexander asked him if he wanted anything, Diogenes replied: 'Only that you step out of my light'. That on the wall facing the fireplace depicts the academy of the Greek philosopher Plato. They were first hung here, with new 'sandstone' borders, in 1702.

The Diogenes Room, which is named after the tapestry depicting the ancient Greek philosopher Diogenes

The Damask Bedchamber

Within the late 17th-century house, the State Bed was the most dramatic way to display your wealth and status. The towering proportions, rich fabrics and elaborate canopy or tester (now very fragile) all ensured that it was the focus for the state apartment. Appropriately for Dyrham, the bed is in the Anglo-Dutch style of the designer Daniel Marot, whom William of Orange had brought to England in 1694. It was made, perhaps by Francis Lapierre about 1704, from crimson and yellow velvet with an interior of sprigged satin. The bed stood originally in Dyrham's grandest bedroom, which was on the floor immediately above, until sold in 1912 to the Lady Lever Art Gallery, which has kindly loaned it back since 1965. It has never been slept in.

The suite of *c.*1680 walnut chairs was given red wool case covers to protect them from the damaging effects of sunlight.

Flowerpiece by Nicholas van Veerendael in the Damask Bedchamber

The Damask Bedchamber

The Closet

A Vauxhall mirror of
*c.*1690 hangs above the
marquetry table in the
Damask Bedchamber

The Closet

In this intimate room in 1703 you could sit on one of the four cushioned stools, write at the 'Japan Writing Table', or look at the '2 great & ten little Pictures'.

You may also have taken chocolate here. Hence perhaps the mid-17th-century painting of a cocoa tree. Blathwayt had interests in Jamaica, which was the chief British source of chocolate after 1655. At that time it was taken in liquid form, as a hot drink combined with eggs and spices. Pepys used it as a cure for indigestion. Among the Dyrham crockery in 1703 were a 'chocolate pott' and '9 plain and 9 ribbed chocolate cupps'. The Blathwayts still had a sweet tooth in 1777, when bills show that a pound of chocolate cost them 5s 6d (27.5p).

The Back Closet

In 1703 the walls of this little room were covered with red hangings, but it was virtually unfurnished. It may have contained a close-stool (lavatory) or chamber-pot, which could easily be removed and emptied by servants using the narrow stairs which lie just beyond its inner door.

Walk down the stairs into the Servants' Quarters.

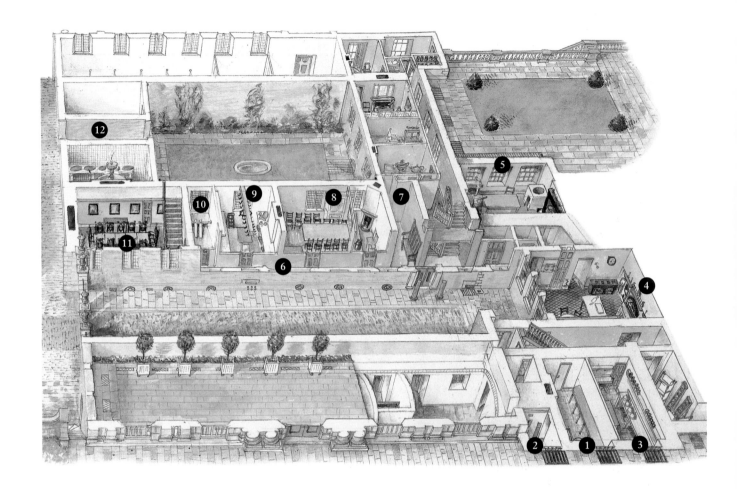

1 Bakehouse Larder

2 Bakehouse

3 Cold Meat Larder

4 Kitchen

5 Scullery (*closed*)

6 Servants' Hall Passage

7 Still Room (*closed*)

8 Servants' Hall (*closed*)

9 Wet Larder

10 Lamp Room (*closed*)

11 Tenants' Hall

12 Dairy

The Servants' Quarters

In 1844–5 Colonel Blathwayt completely modernised the servants' quarters, constructing a new kitchen and removing the entire top floor from the service wing, which had been built in 1698. It is his arrangement which you see today. It may look large and complex, but in fact the Colonel's aim was to reduce the domestic offices to a more manageable (and affordable) size. He ran Dyrham more like a large farmhouse than a Victorian mansion.

In 1851 the household was controlled by the butler, the 53-year-old Patrick Connor, who had come to Dyrham from Ireland with the Colonel. The housekeeper was the 60-year-old Margery McGuckon. There were seven other servants. Ten years later, Mr Connor and Mrs McGuckon were still in service (although Mrs McGuckon would admit only to being 65). The rest had all changed and comprised: footman, messenger, lady's maid, cook, three housemaids, dairymaid, kitchenmaid, and nurse (the Colonel now had a two-year-old granddaughter, Mary).

The Bakehouse Larder

In 1871 this room held a store of flour in a large bin, and a dough-trough (pronounced 'trow'), a deep wooden box in which the flour was kneaded with warm water, yeast and salt. Having been turned out into deep bowls, the dough was then placed in the warm proving oven in the Bakehouse next door, until it had doubled in size. It was then returned to the Bakehouse Larder to be 'knocked back' and kneaded once more before being made up into loaves and replaced in the proving oven to rise once more. Only then was it placed in the oven to bake.

The Bakehouse

Here all the bread was made for the entire household in a bread oven installed by Messrs Stothert & Walker of Bath; the proving oven is immediately below.

The Cold Meat Larder

The Victorians knew the importance of storing cooked and raw meats completely separate from one another. This room was a 'dry larder' for cooked meats, pies and potted meats, and probably for the bread, cheese and eggs required for household use.

The Kitchen

Until the 1840s, the Kitchen was where the Tenants' Hall now is. By building this new kitchen, Colonel Blathwayt brought the cooking area some 25 metres closer to his Dining Room, ensuring that all his food was served fresh and hot.

For the actual cooking, three arched fireplaces were built against the south wall. All the ranges were made by Stothert & Walker. The left-hand fireplace has a pastry oven heated by its own furnace. In the next arch is a large roasting range, its fire being made larger or smaller by winding the two thick iron 'cheeks' and their boiling rings in or out, using rack-and-pinion mechanisms inside both of the hobs. When in use, the hot air rushing up the chimney turned a large propeller mounted within the flue, which then operated the smoke-jack gearing mounted on the chimneybreast.

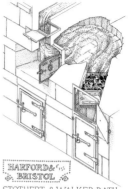

HARFORD & BRISTOL

STOTHERT & WALKER. BATH.

Flames from a firebox to the right swirled around the brick-lined interior of the oven, leaving by way of the open oven door and up, through a damper which controlled the draught, into a flue channelled across the top of the oven, into the old chimneystack. When the masonry was really hot, the fire was raked out into the ashpit beneath, along with any ashes which remained in the oven itself, and the oven door closed to retain the heat

The indoor servants in the late 19th century

The lady's maid Annie Gerry with 'Dandy' around 1905-9

From the Kitchen, the door in the south-west corner leads firstly into a short passage fitted with store and pantry cupboards, and then into the Nursery Staircase.

The Servants' Hall Passage

Since the Servants' Hall lay along this passage, it was the ideal location for the bell system. Each of the main family rooms had a bell-pull, which was connected by a copper wire to one of the bells mounted on the left side of the passage. Those from the servants' rooms were mounted on the right. Once the bell had been pulled, it rang for a few seconds, after which the pendulum beneath continued to swing so that the servants could both hear and see who required their services. In addition, bell-pulls at each side of the Servants' Hall door, marked 'MALE' and 'FEMALE', rang bells up in the footmen's and female servants' bedrooms, to wake them each morning, or in case of any night-time emergency. The painted labels preserve the Victorian room names, including the Ghost Chamber, which, rather surprisingly, was being used as a children's bedroom in 1871.

The niche with the grotesque face set into the passage wall just beyond the Servants' Hall was inserted here in the 1840s. It probably came from William Blathwayt's bathroom or *bagnio* (from the Italian for bath), which occupied the space now filled by the Bakehouse and Bakehouse Larder. This was an oval room lined with Dutch tiles similar to those in the Dairy, where he could enjoy a steam bath or wash in a lead-lined bath.

The Wet Larder

This room has always served as a larder, being refitted in the 1840s as a 'wet larder' for raw and salt meat and game. The ventilation duct above the door ensured that there was a constant draught to keep the room cool and fresh. Game would be hung from the Dutch crown fixed to the centre of the main beam. More game, along with bacon and hams, was hung from the other hooks which line the sides of the beam. Various joints of meat would be kept on pottery dishes on the cool stone shelves, while salt meats, and those in the process of being salted, were kept in four brown earthenware pans probably stored beneath the shelves at floor level.

The Tenants' Hall

Until the 1840s this was the Great Kitchen. On rent days, the leading tenants on the Blathwayts' extensive estate dined here at three dining tables linked to form a single long table in the centre of the room.

You can still see traces of the gallery which was constructed around two walls so that the footmen could reach their bedrooms in the adjoining wing.

The Dairy

In the 1840s, the Dairy was moved from the southern end of the service wing into what had previously been the scullery or 'little kitchen stove room', which had had a roasting range and baking oven. The fine Delft tiles seem to have been stripped off the walls of the old dairy, and relaid here at the same time. The large stone fountain was installed in 1846 to keep the Dairy cool and moist.

(*Opposite*) In 1861 this was the domain of Frances Perry, the 24-year-old dairymaid. She provided milk and cream for the house, storing them in fourteen shallow milk pans, which were set out on the marble shelves. There was no equipment for making either butter or cheese, which appear to have been bought ready-made

Dyrham the Seat of William Blathwait Esq.

The Garden and Park

William Blathwayt's Garden

William Blathwayt chose a royal architect for his new house, and he also turned to the royal gardener, George London, for advice on the garden that was to surround it. His house has survived almost intact; his garden has vanished almost entirely. But, fortunately, a bird's-eye view drawn by Johannes Kip gives us a remarkably detailed and accurate picture of what it looked like in 1710.

Blathwayt knew William and Mary's famous garden at Het Loo, and like the furnishings of the house, his garden was mostly Dutch in style. However, Holland is a flat country, and the terrain around Dyrham is not. To create even terraces suitable for formal parterres and canals, huge amounts of earth had to be moved. 'When will this levelling be at an end?' Blathwayt wrote in despair in 1698. But the natural geography also provided superb vantage points from which to look down on the garden. The whole design was laid out around the doors of the East and West Halls. From the west door four rows of parterres led to a set of grand gates. On the slope above the parterres were the Slope Garden, which was designed to be seen from what is now the Dining Room, and a walled terrace, which still survives, but is now a deer sanctuary. Below the parterres two mill ponds were turned into rectangular ponds separated by a cascade and fountain, and there was also a kitchen garden.

The Dyrham park is full of natural springs, of which London made particularly clever use on the east side of the house. The statue of Neptune, carved by Claude David, marks the spot where a fountain rose six metres into the air. The water then flowed down a cascade of 225 steps to another fountain and finally into a long canal aligned with the centre of the Orangery. Something of the effect can still be seen at Chatsworth in Derbyshire. On the hillside above the central parterres were four more terraces and above them, a 'wilderness' – woodland through which walks had been cut.

Blathwayt used his connections with Virginia to provide Virginia pines and flowering oaks and other exotic species for the park. His head gardener, Thomas Hurnall, brought packets of seeds from the garden at Longleat in Wiltshire, where London was also working, and bills survive for lemons, pyracantha and laurustinus. In the winter, the Orangery was filled with 'all manner of fine Greens, as Oranges, Lemons, Mirtles &c. set in the most beautiful order'.

The same view around 1790, when William Blathwayt's formal garden had almost completely disappeared, to be replaced by open parkland

In this Canal several Sorts of Fish are confin'd, as Trout, Perch, Carp, &c. of a very large Size, and tho' it is deep, yet the Water is so transparent that you may easily discover the scaley Residents, even those of the smallest Dimensions: And this Canal is so very much frequented in the Summer, that the Fish will not be disturb'd at your Approach: but are almost as tame as the Swans, (two whereof continually waft themselves with Grandeur in this Canal) which will not scruple to take an uncommon Feeding from your Hands.

The garden theorist Stephen Switzer writing in 1718 about Blathwayt's garden

William Blathwayt's extraordinarily elaborate garden, as recorded by Johannes Kip in 1710

The Garden and Park Today

The complexity of Blathwayt's garden would have required a huge staff to maintain, and by the time of his death in 1717, its formal style was already going out of fashion. Thanks to the inertia of his descendants, the garden survived into the second half of the 18th century, but by 1779 one visitor was commenting that the water gardens, 'which were made at a great expense, are much neglected and going to decay', and by 1791 they had been 'reconciled to modern Taste' – that is, swept away.

The garden and park we see today were largely the work of Charles Harcourt-Masters, the builder of the Holborne of Menstrie Museum in Bath, who was called in by William Blathwayt IV around 1800 to remodel what was left of the builder's garden. He moved the main entrance drive (the present approach) to the east of the house to take advantage of the improvement of the Bath–Stroud road. Open grassland, grazed by Dyrham's deer, now swept right up to the house in the style of 'Capability' Brown. He also planted clumps of cedars contrasting with broad-leaved chestnuts and beeches on the surrounding slopes to frame the famous view from the drive. To the west of the house, he created a smaller and more practical garden. Although his elms succumbed to Dutch elm disease in the 1970s, many of the mature trees in the park are his.

Harcourt-Masters may have been carrying out plans drawn up by the leading garden designer Humphry Repton, who paid a visit to Dyrham in September 1800

The garden to the south-west of the house

and left a design for a summer-house and a bill for his ideas. Between 1800 and 1804 the park was extended to its present size, but little more seems to have been done during the 19th century.

Today, Dyrham is most famous for its trees, which include mature examples of the Tulip Tree, Holm Oak and mulberry. But its long horticultural tradition is maintained in the Orangery, where the citrus plants overwinter in tubs, as they did in William Blathwayt's time. The south and west walls of the house also provide a sun-trap for *Solanum crispum* 'Glasnevin', *Magnolia delavayi* and myrtles. The bones of Blathwayt's garden can still be glimpsed in the ponds to the west of the stable block, and the original central drive still shows through the grass in times of drought. Recent investigation has revealed that the foundations of the formal garden lie not far below the surface.

An 18th-century stone, which now stands in the Orangery

Deep borders and yew hedges front the 13th-century church

Life at Dyrham

Mary Wynter, the heiress to Dyrham, who married William Blathwayt in 1686

Thomas Povey, Blathwayt's uncle, who helped to steer his career and form his artistic taste. Many of the books, furniture and china at Dyrham came from Povey's collection

Early History

The history of Dyrham goes back to Roman times, but the early owners – principally, the Russel and Denys families – have left few traces here. The large canopied monument in Dyrham church is to George Wynter, who, with his brother, Sir William, bought the manor and park of Dyrham in 1571. Together, the Wynter brothers ran the Elizabethan navy as Clerk of the Ships and Master of Naval Ordnance. George helped to finance Sir Francis Drake's voyage round the world in 1577, in which his son, John, took part, and which almost ruined the family. Sir William played a leading role in the defeat of the Spanish Armada in 1588, proposing the fireship attack which scattered the enemy fleet off Calais. The estate subsequently passed to George's great-granddaughter, Mary Wynter. It was with her marriage in 1686 to William Blathwayt that the story of Dyrham as you see it today really begins.

Thomas Povey (?1618–?1700)

To understand William Blathwayt, you must first understand his uncle, Thomas Povey, who guided his nephew's career and artistic tastes. With the restoration of Charles II in 1660, Povey was made treasurer to the King's brother, the Duke of York. He also served as secretary of the Committee for Foreign Plantations, which oversaw the lucrative new colonies in the West Indies. However, he was not the most competent of civil servants. When the diarist Samuel Pepys inherited one of his posts, he found the accounts in a complete muddle, complaining, 'The simple Povey,

of all the most ridiculous fools that I ever saw attend to business'. This did not stop Pepys from enjoying Povey's hospitality at his splendidly furnished London house in Lincoln's Inn Fields. Pepys particularly admired his neatly arranged wine cellar and his fine collection of contemporary Dutch paintings. Povey was known for his formal manners and way of speaking, and as a man of learning, who was elected a founder member of the Royal Society. The diarist John Evelyn called him 'a nice contriver of all elegancies'.

William Blathwayt I (?1649–1717)

William Blathwayt's contemporaries considered him a methodical, but dull and pedantic man. The poet Matthew Prior nicknamed him 'the elephant' for the ponderousness of his jokes. But there was another side to his character. He loved books and music, collecting rare volumes in many languages and playing the violin himself.

Blathwayt followed his uncle into the civil service, but was altogether more efficient and successful. Before he was 20, he was working as private secretary to the British Ambassador in The Hague, and quickly became fluent in Dutch. In the ambassador's absence, he took over full responsibility for the office and was considered 'very exceeding ready and serviceable in all things conducing to his Majesty's service'. He later travelled across Europe with the Duke of Richmond, finally returning to England in 1673, where he won the respect of the King by finding a doctor who could cure a sickly niece.

As clerk to the Privy Council from

1678, he found himself moving in the highest political circles. In 1683 he bought the post of Secretary at War, becoming effectively the administrative head of the army. Blathwayt loyally sided with James II in 1688, when the King was deposed by the Dutch William of Orange. Not surprisingly, he was dismissed from his main government posts, but William found that he could not do without such a competent Dutch-speaking official and reinstated Blathwayt only three months later. He accompanied the King on his frequent visits back to Holland, and was given his own apartment in the royal palace at Het Loo. He also accompanied the King during his wars against the French in Flanders.

In his late thirties, Blathwayt began to think about getting married and becoming a country gentleman. He found a suitable bride in Mary Wynter, who was 36 (old for a bride at that time), but heiress to the Dyrham estate. Negotiating the complex marriage contract took three months, but finally the couple was married in Dyrham church at Christmas 1686. Over the next five years they had four children, three of whom survived infancy, but in November 1691 Mary died. What had begun as a marriage of convenience seems to have grown into a union of true affection: Blathwayt never remarried, and reverently preserved her hair brushes and combs. Undaunted, he pressed on with rebuilding Dyrham.

William Blathwayt, the builder of Dyrham: 'A very proper, handsome person, very dexterous in business' (John Evelyn)

The centre of the east front. The stone eagle – the Blathwayt crest – was hoisted onto the parapet in 1705

Building the House

By 1416 there was already a house on this sheltered spot, set down in the hollow of the valley and close to the ancient parish church. In the early 16th century it was extended or rebuilt with an extra courtyard by two generations of the Denys family. When the antiquary John Leland visited around 1535, he praised it as 'a fayre maner place'. The 1601 inventory lists 22 rooms, thirteen of which were used by servants. The Little Parlour contained a virginals and 'one chayre for a childe'. An estate map of 1689 seems to show a house of many gables approached from the west.

When William Blathwayt had paid his first visit in 1686, he had not been impressed: 'I am afraid there will be a necessity of building a new house at Dirham or being at a very great expense in repairing this.' Blathwayt had good reason to be careful about money. His father had left him an estate 'extremely embroiled and impaired', and Blathwayt himself was lucky to hang on to his lucrative government jobs after the overthrow of James II in 1688, which had also depleted his wife's inheritance. Because he depended on income rather than investments to finance the rebuilding of Dyrham, he had to proceed cautiously. Rather than demolishing the Tudor house, he retained its core, and added new ranges in stages, as the money became available.

In 1692 Blathwayt was appointed William III's acting Secretary of State, with a salary of £2,200. He could now start work on a new west range, which contains the Walnut Staircase and the first-floor apartment. His architect was a mysterious Mr S. Hauduroy, who may have been a Huguenot (Protestant) exile from France. Certainly, the style of the range was French, resembling a Paris town house of the period, with an enclosed courtyard in front, flanked by low wings containing nurseries and a covered passage to the church. The golden stone came from the Tolldean quarry about a mile away. Some of the craftsmen were also local, including Richard West of Corsham, who was the main building contractor. However, London craftsmen were called in to do the finer work, such as the plasterwork ceilings (now gone) and the architectural panelling in the Balcony Room. Blathwayt watched anxiously from London, as the delays, and the costs, mounted, firing off frequent stiff letters to his agent, 'Cozen Watkins'. By 1694, however, this range was finished.

Four years later, he could afford to add a large new stable block to the west range. It was grouped around two courtyards with stalls for 26 horses, new kitchens, brew-house, laundry and bedrooms above for the servants. (The top floor was removed in the 1840s.) The block was designed by Edward Wilcox, who was foreman to the King's architect, William Talman, and who had built new stables at Kensington Palace a few years before.

In 1698 Blathwayt was appointed to the Board of Trade with a salary of £1,000. He decided to demolish the remains of the Tudor house and build a new east range with a state apartment on an altogether grander scale than his first efforts. As a senior government official, he had access to the best architects in the country, and so turned to Talman himself. The stone came from the Oldfield quarry near Bath, and had to be dragged here over Lansdown

Blathwayt filled his new house with blue-and-white Delft china

The west front, which was Blathwayt's first addition to the house, in 1692–4

Hill. Perhaps partly for this reason, work did not start till March 1700, and the carved Blathwayt eagle was not finally lifted onto the roof until 1705. The new range was in the baroque style of Talman's great rival, Christopher Wren, which was already falling out of fashion. It was also indebted to some of the most admired buildings in Europe – the baroque *palazzi* of Genoa. However, the source got slightly garbled in translation: the local masons inserted the first-floor balustrades under the wrong windows.

Blathwayt furnished his new apartments primarily in the Dutch style, commissioning a vast state bed in the Anglo-Dutch manner of the King's favourite designer, Daniel Marot, and buying Dutch pictures, books and furniture from his uncle. During his continental travels he also picked up blue-and-white Delft china and Dutch leather hangings.

In 1701 Blathwayt extended the east range with an orangery, which formed the focus for his vast formal garden (see p.23) and was one of the first large greenhouses in England. In thirteen years, Blathwayt had transformed Dyrham from a rambling Tudor manor-house into a great baroque mansion fit to entertain a monarch. But his patron, William III died in 1702, and under Queen Anne his career went into gradual decline. He lost his jobs as Secretary of State, Secretary at War (apparently, for cracking a joke that backfired) and at the Board of Trade, and spent his last years in rather embittered retirement at Dyrham.

Penelope and Jeremiah Crane's son, William, who inherited Dyrham in 1817, when he changed his surname to Blathwayt

William Blathwayt IV and his wife Frances. She survived until 1844, almost causing the break-up of Dyrham

The 18th Century

William Blathwayt I was the first and only member of the family to sit in Parliament, and his successors seem to have been content with the quiet country life of Gloucestershire squires. His son, William II, who inherited in 1717, made few changes to the house beyond putting up new yellow curtains in the Dining Room.

The third William, who succeeded in 1742, ran short of money and in 1765 was forced to sell one of the jewels of the picture collection, Murillo's *An Urchin mocking an Old Woman eating Polenta*, but fortunately his younger brother was able to buy it back and so it stayed in the family. Nor could he afford to keep up the builder's elaborate formal garden, which in any case had fallen out of fashion. The terraces were allowed to decay gradually, to be replaced by open grassland, which was easier to maintain.

William IV repaired the 100-year-old house after he inherited in 1787. Family scandal disrupted his quiet existence in 1789, when his sister Penelope eloped to Scotland with a bankrupt Bristol man, Jeremiah Crane – 'a rash and precipitate step', according to her uncle. Five years later, the couple had a son, again named William, whom they gave away to be brought up at Dyrham as the childless William IV's heir.

William IV was not a popular figure with some of his tenants, and the 1790s were a troubled time in the Gloucestershire countryside. In March 1795 600 of them gathered in a nearby wood and burnt an effigy of him. The militia was called out, but by deferring their rent payments, he was able to negotiate 'a happy & peaceable termination of this unpleasant business', as a friend put it.

Colonel George William Blathwayt (1797–1871)

The Colonel was the son of the rector of Dyrham, who was William Blathwayt IV's younger step-brother. In 1814 at the age of 17 he joined the 23rd Light Dragoons and was involved in putting down disturbances among the Lancashire cotton workers. The following year, he fought at the Battle of Waterloo, observing Napoleon's movements through his telescope.

Although the Colonel barely knew Dyrham, having lived most of his life in Ireland and having dined only twice in the house, he was determined to save the place, when its future was threatened in 1844. After William IV's nephew and heir, William Crane (who had changed his name to Blathwayt on inheriting), had died

Colonel George William Blathwayt, who rescued Dyrham in 1844 after years of neglect

Dance card for a Dyrham ball

Dyrham Park about 1845, when Colonel Blathwayt was restoring the house and modernising the servants' quarters

childless in 1839, the estate reverted to William IV's widow, Frances, who had remarried an Admiral Douglas. When she died in 1844, the house was left to the Colonel, but the contents went to Frances's Douglas relations, who had neglected the place and threatened to strip it bare. Although not a wealthy man, he took out a huge loan of £50,000 to buy back the furniture and pictures and repair the house. Between 1844 and 1846 he spent £23,000 on restoring Dyrham, laying 66 tons of lead on the roof, installing central heating (then a very novel invention) and nine new WCs, and rationalising the rambling servants' quarters. The family pictures were all taken down so that the main rooms could be repainted and replastered. He also modernised many of the cottages on the estate.

Dyrham was saved, but at a considerable cost to the Colonel. In 1858 he was still paying a third of his income just to service the interest on his loan. Even so, he enjoyed the life of a no-nonsense High Tory landowner, and Dyrham was a welcoming place, with regular dances and house parties twice a month. When he died in 1871 aged 74 after falling from a ladder, all the shops in Bath closed for the day as a mark of respect. Tenants on the estate carried his coffin the short distance from the west door to the church, and he was buried in the churchyard beneath a willow tree brought from St Helena, where Napoleon had spent his last years.

Anne, Lady Islington, who rented Dyrham from 1938 to 1946 and redecorated several of the main rooms. In her youth (when this charcoal portrait by J.S. Sargent was drawn), she had belonged to the intellectual circle of aristocrats known as the 'Souls', and she developed a talent for restoring old houses. In 1947 James Lees-Milne described her as 'very active and bustling … outspoken, amusing, hard and thoroughly Edwardian'

(*Right*) The view from the entrance drive, with Claude David's statue of Neptune – one of the few surviving elements from William Blathwayt's garden

The 20th Century

In 1899 the Colonel's younger son, Wynter Blathwayt, inherited the estate, having – in the Dyrham tradition of younger sons – worked as the local rector for most of his life. He was 74 at the time, and so passed the running of the estate on to his son, Robert. As money was again short, Robert was obliged to sell the greatest of the Dutch paintings, Hobbema's *Wooded Landscape* (now in the Frick Collection in New York) for £9870. This paid for vital repairs to the house and for putting in electricity.

Robert had no children, but was still touched by the grief of the First World War. His cousin, Henry, was killed in action at the Battle of Cambrai in 1917. Henry's wife, Elizabeth, was staying at Dyrham when the news came, and for the rest of her life she could not bear to hear the screech of the Dyrham peacocks, as it brought back that moment.

In 1936 Dyrham passed to Elizabeth's son, Christopher, who two years later decided to rent it out to Anne, Lady Islington, the widow of a local MP and Governor-general of New Zealand. She made substantial changes to the historic interiors, moving chimneypieces around and repainting the Drawing Room and Walnut Staircase in lighter tones. Worse almost happened in 1939, when the nursery wing caught fire, but fortunately the main part of the house was saved.

During the Second World War, in which Christopher Blathwayt won the Military Cross, the house was used as a nursery for children evacuated from London. When Lady Islington gave up the lease in 1946, Dyrham's future looked bleak. Much of the house was shut up, and on one occasion sheep were found wandering through the Great Hall. The family decided to give up the house with mixed feelings, as Cecily Blathwayt explained to Lord Methuen in 1954: 'Dear Dyrham, we love it – it's a person – but an exacting one.' In 1956 the house and garden were acquired by the Ministry of Works, using the National Land Fund, which had been set up in 1946 to save places of national importance as a memorial to the dead of the Second World War. After a major campaign of repairs, Dyrham was transferred to the National Trust in 1961. The 110-hectare (272-acre) park, with its ancient herd of deer, was purchased in 1976 with a grant from the National Heritage Memorial Fund.